POEMS FOR ANOTHER TIME

JASON HOLT

ANAPHORA LITERARY PRESS

QUANAH, TEXAS

ANAPHORA LITERARY PRESS
1108 W 3rd Street
Quanah, TX 79252
https://anaphoraliterary.com

Book design by Anna Faktorovich, Ph.D.

Published in 2021 by Anaphora Literary Press

Poems for Another Time
Jason Holt—1st edition.

Library of Congress Control Number: 2021900027

Library Cataloging Information
Holt, Jason, 1971-, author.
    Poems for another time / Jason Holt
    72 p. ; 9 in.
    ISBN 979-8-590155-35-4 (softcover : alk. paper)
    ISBN 978-1-68114-555-6 (hardcover : alk. paper)
    Amazon ASIN (e-book)
1. Poetry—Canadian—General.
2. Poetry—Subjects & Themes—Death, Grief, Loss.
3. Poetry—Subjects & Themes—Love & Erotica.
PN6099-6110: Collections of general literature: Poetry
808.817: Humorous poetry

CONTENTS

In Writing

Nothing Is About You   7
Pointful   8
Leaning In   9
Antinomes   10
No Holds Uncertain   11
Put Me up a Peg   12
Elusion   13
Seventeen Syllables   14
Worse Fates Than to Remain Unsung   15
For Petting of Such Praise   16
Ache for Any Evidence   17
Living Down to It   18
Definition of Virtue   19

Requiem for a Father

Decline   21
Imminence   22
Twilight   23
Cremation   24
Aftermath   25
Almost   26
Beyond   27

Apothegmic Interlude

All In   29
Propinquity   30
Hebetation   31
Debit Where Due   32
Institutions   33
Integrity   34
Existential Equation   35
If You Want to Know Someone Well   36
Suicide   37
Silence   38

Judge a Book   39
All the World   40
People Who Live in the Sunlight   41

Well Alone
No One into You   43
She Takes Delight in All the World but Me   44
What It Doesn't Mean   45
Only When We're Not Getting Along   46
Inhospitality   47
Homeward Walk at Dusk   48
However Low My Hopes   49
A Love so Sharp   50
Inquisite   51
The Avails of Love   52
116 Converted   53
What Strikes and Strikes Again   54
That Sundappled Day   55

Their Currents Turn Awry
In Her Style   57
Good Better Good Enough   58
When in Doubt   59
Inspired by Asian Philosophy   60
Happy Marriage   61
Elizabethan Plays   62
Before Floating My Boat   63
Marooned   64
All for Naught   65
Austin Variations   66
Unexpected Wind   67
A Little Shortwinded   68
A Veritable Who Cares   69
Waning Poetic   70

For Astrid Brunner

In Writing

Nothing Is About You

remember
nothing
is about you
the wisdom
in such negation
looming
small and sweet
cupped
in both hands
like a match

Pointful

pointless
versus
pointful
selfassertion
and the wisdom
to know
not straddle
but stand
on one foot

Leaning In

I plan to lean in
to the coffee
for a while
because
life

Antinomes

everything
is something
and nothing
is anything
both true
together
a pair
of dice
of legs

No Holds Uncertain

I'd like
to tap out now
please
not that we have
that rule here
nothing
so constitutive
in such
no holds
uncertain

Put Me up a Peg

take me down
another peg
sure
but couldn't you wait
till someone
puts me up a peg
first

Elusion

that was not
sunbathing
it was a game
of hide and seek
and I lost

Seventeen Syllables

the blade
that thinks itself
a knife
but grass
yet tears
a hasty finger

Worse Fates Than to Remain Unsung

are there worse fates
than to remain unsung
when lakes and rivers
rest and flow their ways
where immanent
or mutable undone
identity so thwarted
through delays
or haste truncating form
that suits his mark
the signature unseen
in light or dark

For Petting of Such Praise

oh what tricks
I would perform
for petting
of such praise
with status quo
or in reform
in clarity
or haze

Ache for Any Evidence

easy to imagine
sure
the neckbrushing lips
of a revived
if long discounted
ardor
one of those
delicate cynicisms
that ache
for any evidence
to brush against
and kill it

Living Down to It

admittedly I was
living down
to other people's
lack of interest

Definition of Virtue

virtue
is learning
to be
productive
when
you're being
ignored

Requiem for a Father

Decline

have I said enough
or all I have to
father
such an address
wry inkling
that familiar smile
on lips
that hate to register
the pain
the bleeding
that just won't stop
despite the tube's removal
that rare aggressive
form of cancer
swelling all around
even as it drains
your throat
your voice
once eager to perform
now but remembered
as I lean
to strain at every whisper
though nothing left
remains to say
flickers expectation

Imminence

the whiteness
of the frozen lake
the lapping
of the flooding lake
toward
the basement door

the fineness
of my father's hair
as careful
with the unfamiliar task
I run the clippers

a guard for him
but none for me
against what swells within
a haircut
for a dying man
not quite
without regret

Twilight

the strains
of rough music
relaxing me
through waves
my father
like his
elsewise son
settling into
setting into
twilight's
closing eyes

Cremation

when I turned
the four dials
on the oven
to begin
my father's cremation
I wasn't sure
whether I should feel
like luke skywalker
or some nameless nazi
instead
of how I did
and how much better
I would have
if I'd had the words
to match

Aftermath

scattering exactly one year later
the ashes in the woods
along the twelfth fairway
to the left the distant clubhouse
to the right close inevitable
the overwater thirteenth
where young I swimming
for errant summer golf balls
saw and heard absorbing full
his face looming over the rowboat
such astonished disappointment
that I didn't know then
as only sometimes now
how to surface dive

Almost

I reach out
again
again
almost touching

Beyond

be wistful
for
those never taken
grasps
that always fluttered
reach
as if
in spoken
ghostly reassurance
jase

Apothegmic Interlude

All In

it's all
in
the preposition

Propinquity

propinquity
is license

Hebetation

he who
hebetates
is lost

Debit Where Due

debit
where debit
is due

Institutions

institutions
inevitably
become what
they are not

Integrity

integrity
is being
what one is
not what
one is not

Existential Equation

beauvoir

=

sartre

+

hume

If You Want to Know Someone Well

if you want
to know someone well
find out
what they'd die for
if you want
to know them really well
find out
what gets them hot

Suicide

suicide
is not
a viable
strategy

Silence

silence
is a kind
of affirmation
in itself

Judge a Book

judge a book
by not its cover
but its title

All the World

all the world's
a page

People Who Live in the Sunlight

people who live
in the sunlight
shouldn't throw shade

Well Alone

No One into You

whoever she is
she's no one
into you
right now
however long
the marriage
may have been
or last

She Takes Delight in All the World but Me

she takes delight in all the world but me
though once it was the converse in the main
the giving in an arching revelry
as if to gripping purpose entertain
the reach of memories that less would sting
if not so bold they drove this passion on
the highway as a rover's offering
become a homeward-bounding autobahn
a call now taken sprightening the voice
as from a kitchen chore I ease my rest
this steaming cup for company my choice
as twilight stumbles darker gray and blessed
in wounding from its etymology
it pulses will to blind philosophy

What It Doesn't Mean

it's okay
I know what sex
doesn't mean to you
the aching loss of gain
of some all resolutive self
that elusive chord
you know how to play
but just not quite
well enough

Only When We're Not Getting Along

I only worry
this stubborn pustule
on my chest
when we're
not getting along
I wonder
if it
will ever heal

Inhospitality

it's not a great day
out there
it's not a great day
in here
for that mind
or matter
which
of the two colds
more inhospitable
[*slam*]

Homeward Walk at Dusk

if the car isn't there
I'll sink
but if it is
I'll sink faster and further
all my efforts tightening
around my own throat
much as I'd
give up breathing
to box with tissue paper
her brittle what's now

However Low My Hopes

however low
I set my hopes
for this relationship
you keep
disappointing them

A Love so Sharp

a love so sharp
a hate so sweet
a poem long
a poem neat
a vodka rocks
a vodka neat
a love so sharp
a hate so sweet

Inquisite

vulnerable
in a way
that could be
so exquisite
but mostly
is all too
inquisite
instead

The Avails of Love

living
off
the avails
of love

116 Converted

let me not
to the marriage
of true impediments
admit mind[1]

---
1   Suggested in conversation with Astrid Brunner.

What Strikes and Strikes Again

pulverized
in all the work
that word entails
my heart again
my heart again
on offer
as though it never
learned or took
a lesson or advice
from what strikes
and strikes again
as beating
beating
beating

That Sundappled Day

that sundappled day
on that roofdeck
torn down years ago now
from your father's cabin
beside the long stretch
of mudflats waiting for the tide

not the first time
or the best
or the first time sweet
with archmade grip
and deepest into eyes
to as you say touch souls
nor even first as claiming right
we made a love
whose memories persist us
in its thoughts
as in our hearts persist
we it and all the sun wherein

this overcast now
in a later summer languoring
no lesser more
our slim and yearn
our partial tan and slumber

Their Currents Turn Awry

In Her Style

since she merits praise
though lighter or darker
let's our glasses raise
to dorothy parker

Good Better Good Enough

good better
good enough
never let it
get too rough
until
your good
is better
and your better
good enough

When in Doubt

when in doubt
no bout
when in bout
no doubt

Inspired by Asian Philosophy

wuxin
mushin
flow
how
chi ki
of me
though

Happy Marriage

I like you svelte
and I like you chubby
'cause you're my wife
and I'm your hubby

Elizabethan Plays

come live with me and be my sweet
and we will all the pleasures greet
such introductions more than meat
to feed our hungry passions

come live with me and be my twist
and we will all the pleasures grist
for milling us the grindstone kissed
us roughly as we like it

come live with me and be my lass
and we the pleasures all will pass
from each to each between amass
to comfort through the years

come live with me and be my spouse
and keep the pleasures all in-house
then deluges of time won't douse
this fire or its embers

Before Floating My Boat

whatever
rocks
your box

Marooned

a distant couple
walking
in matching
maroon jackets

I guess
if you're going
to be marooned
it's better
to be marooned
together

All for Naught

all for naught
and naught for all

Austin Variations

how to do things
with words

how to do words
with things

how to word things
with do

Unexpected Wind

tuchus
by surprise

A Little Shortwinded

I guess
after all
I'm
a little
shortwinded

A Veritable Who Cares

at the very last
conference
I may ever attend
it was
a veritable
who cares
of canadian
philosophy

Waning Poetic

better
I think
to wane
poetic

OTHER ANAPHORA LITERARY PRESS TITLES

Beloved Combrades
By: Yermiyahu Ahron Taub

Notes for Further Research
By: Molly Kirschner

Falling and Other Stories
By: Ben Stoltzfus

The Visit
By: Michael G. Casey

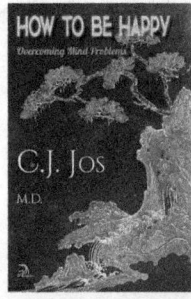

How to Be Happy
By: C. J. Jos

A Dying Breed
By: Scott Duff

Love in the Cretaceous
By: Howard W. Robertson

*Emergence: The Role of
Mindfulness in Creativity*
By: Rosie Rosenzweig

CPSIA information can be obtained
at www.ICGtesting.com
Printed in the USA
BVHW031020120121
597543BV00004BA/67